T0353708

RETIRE LIKE A
ROCK STAR

RETIRE LIKE A ROCK STAR

Introducing the Next Level, Tax Free
Retirement Saving Solution That Eliminates the
7 Deadly Sins of Your 401(k) or IRA

STEPHEN DRAVIN

Rev. date: 02/18/2025

To order additional copies of this book, contact:
Xlibris
844-714-8691
www.Xlibris.com
Orders@Xlibris.com
865654

Contents

Contents

Preface

"I don't care too much for money...
Money can't buy me love"
Lyrics from the Beatles hit, 1965

We all know money can't buy things like health, happiness – or even love! But when it comes to a nicer home, great vacations, the best schools for your children - and on and on - having money *and being able to access it* is pretty darned important.

Yes, *there is a next gen retirement savings solution* that provides you and your family with the money and peace of mind for a financially secure retirement – and ready access to funds long before you call it a career.

A 'Rock Star'... of a different kind

OK, be honest: we all want to be 'rock stars" of a sort! Maybe you can't rock the guitar or drums....and have a screaming audience of fans. But, the superior lifelong savings solution you'll learn about here – will make you a veritable "rock star" in the eyes of your family. After all, you've provided – very well - for your family, now and over a lifetime.

Chapter 1

The 7 Deadly Sins (of other retirement plans)

The traditional retirement plans (IRA, 401(k), Roth) out there are "a good start" – you get tax deferred earnings, (generally) a tax deduction, and often convenient and "easy" ways to invest (i.e. in mutual funds). If it's a 401(k) plan at your employer, it's even more convenient; almost "set it and forget it"... for many years.

However, it's also "easy" to forget some major drawbacks that you'll face – now and later. We call them the "7 deadly sins" and they are:

1. **Taxes** – income in retirement and beforehand too (with early withdrawals) – is at ordinary rates. Deductions may well be lower in retirement years. And, many expect federal income tax rate rises in the future. Penalties may apply as well.

2. **Limited liquidity** – in many cases, amount accessible is very restricted; may have to repay within 5 years (with the 401(k)). Taxes and penalties may also apply.

3. **Market risk** – equity based accounts are subject to full market risk – even with a diversified portfolio of different mutual funds. This risk is particularly striking and feared in years just before or during retirement.

4. **Contribution limits and inflexibility** – relatively low ($5500) in the IRA or Roth (which has major income

1

restrictions too. For high earners, even the 401(k) has contribution restrictions.

Cannot "make up" for contributions not made previous years. Can be a real drawback to those able to afford more contributions later in their career.

As to Roth IRA *income restrictions, note this:*

Married couples filing jointly with a <u>Modified Adjusted Gross Income</u> (MAGI) of $183,000 or less ($116,000 or less for individuals) can contribute the maximum amount of $5,500 to a Roth IRA for 2015. Couples with an MAGI greater than $193,000 ($131,000 for individuals) are ineligible for a Roth IRA. If you are over 50 you may also be able to make a catch up contribution of $1,000 per individual.

5. **RMDs** – "required minimum distributions" (at age 70.5) force one to take out certain percentages every year – with a high penalty for non-compliance. A dreaded requirement for folks with substantial assets who want to maximize their legacies.

6. **Alternative Minimum Taxes and Social Security Taxation** – income from most traditional plan sources contributes to higher AMT and SS taxes

7. **Impact on others of a premature death. Tax implications for beneficiaries**. The Income Tax on the account is payable by Heirs.

2

Chapter 2

What makes this 'strategy' so good?

To say that a product – or anything – is "good" begs the question: "Good compared to what?"

We're going to pull back the curtains and reveal our "solution" in the next chapter... but from now, let's see how "it" compares to well-known retirement plans and approaches.

Listed below are twenty potential positive attributes/benefits of a retirement strategy"

1. Tax deductions 11. No impact on AMT
2. Tax deferral of earnings 12. Useful for College Funding
3. Tax free distributions at retirement 13. No impact on Social Security
4. Easy access/liquidity 14. Creditor protection (certain states)
5. Market like returns 15. NO market risk
6. "Favorable" liquidity 16. More years of distributions –
7. No contribution limits 17. Uses for long term care expenses
8. No Income restrictions 18. Low costs for business owners
9. Inclusion of a death benefit 19. Contribution flexibility
10. "Accelerated" benefits 20. No RMDs

Of all possible retirement plans and approaches, our "favored one" has all but one of the above (it's #1)!

The Roth IRA can claim eight (40%) of the above benefits! The IRA or 401(k) have only 3 of the above. Case studies (see the Resource Center of our website) show significant future income and legacy superiority to the 401(k) or IRA.

Chapter 3

The Next Gen <u>Retirement Savings Solution</u> – in a Nutshell

What's in a name?

Take a breath and suspend for a moment some time honored myths and misconceptions you may harbor. Let's pull back the curtain: that multi-purpose, 401(k) alternative is actually a variant of (yes) permanent cash value life insurance, called "indexed universal life" (IUL). Seriously!

Don't bail just yet! *The only way to get all these benefits is to use a Life Insurance policy.* Sure, this sucks. It feeds into all the myths and misconceptions I used to believe about life insurance: "It's expensive"..."Buy term and invest the difference"... blab blah blah. So, at first, I tuned out.

But then, I asked myself this important question:

"Do I care more about what it's called, or what it can accomplish for me?"

"Say what?" you wonder. I'll repeat: "What is more important to you – what something is called...or what that 'thing' can actually do for you?"

You'll come to see that the benefits are more important than the name.

A truly new kind of "hybrid" life insurance (hint: it's one you'll love)

The IUL is unlike anything you probably know about – this policy is called (excuse the jargon) a "flexible premium, universal life policy". It's a cash accumulation policy ON STEROIDS. It needs to be designed from the ground up to maximize cash accumulation, provide tax free income – and *reduce the death benefit to the bare legal minimum.*

For many, it will outperform their 401(k) or IRA given comparable market returns – and do so by offering many more years of after tax income... and a remaining legacy.

Growth with protection

IULs vary by carrier but all provide for market related (various indexes used) account growth - yet there are no downsides due to market declines (there are costs). *One does not invest in any equity or index directly.* IUL's typically involve "caps" or maximums (in the 12 to 15% area) - the account is able to gain. Then there are "floors" (generally zero), so the account cannot decline due to the market. Account values are reset annually so gains are never given back. It is beyond the scope here to discuss IUL details and benefits; see sources at the end of this article.

IULs and Liquidity – it's tough to beat

The IUL offers some serious extras that are not readily apparent. For one thing, the liquidity allowed here is a big deal. You can access your account values and take out monies using 'loans' that do not have to be repaid and incur no penalties nor taxes; can be taken for any reason without cost either. Need funds for personal reasons, for college funding? Take it! Business or investment opportunities? Go for it.

Earn money... on money you've taken out!

Particularly striking – and most unusual – is the ability to take out monies and still earn market-linked credits (related to the S&P 500 or other indexes) on the amount withdrawn as loans. So, what you earn may exceed the (variable) loan charges. This potential 'spread' is called 'positive arbitrage' and is part of the "secret sauce" that powers the IUL to increased long term tax free income compared to qualified plans.

Your 'exit strategy"

The preferred way to take out monies – before or during retirement is via 'policy loans' that:

- Do not have to be repaid
- do not incur penalties nor taxes IF the policy is designed properly

What's the catch?

There's a few – underwriting, no initial tax deductions and early costs are the prime ones (some others are discussed in the Chapter "Full Disclosure").........but these are often manageable and mitigated by the IULs many long term advantages.

The other catch? Our government, with trillions of debt, can legislate away many of the huge tax advantages of life insurance at any time. Several tax revenue acts of the 1980's did just that (but life insurance remains a great legal tax haven).

Generally speaking, if one had an IUL policy in place, "grandfathering" would allow you to retain those terrific tax breaks into the future.

Chapter 4

2 case study examples

Case 1.

Personals: "Jared M", NJ, 35 year old, married, male, 1 child, age 8,

Total Household income = $165,000,

IT Security Manager, Spouse a receptionist earning $35,000, good health, non-tobacco.

Premiums in: from age 35 to 66, $750 monthly

Initial death benefit = $260K

Total in through age 66 = $288,000

IUL Annualized Performance Estimate = 7.5%

   (long tern historic average)

Distributions age 67 to 92 = $95,100 annually (tax free)

Cash value at end age 66 = $ 935K (tax free)   At 92 = $ 372K (tax free)

Death ben at end of 66 = $ 1.2 mil (tax free)   At 92 = $ 602K (tax free)

Comparison to a 401(k):

- assumed tax rate at retirement = 28%
- Performance in 401(k): assume 8.5% until age 66, then 5.5% after
- Distribute from age 67: equivalent amount to match after tax amount from IUL

Money runs out at age = 78, and no death benefit will be paid.

Case 2

Personals - "Dr. Pamela S", Maryland, 42 years old, female, 2 children, an OB-GYN with two other partners in her practice, married, good health, non-tobacco, total household income = $425K. Husband a teacher earning $65,000. She was contributing to a 401(k) plan at her practice. Reduced those contributions and took on an IUL solution that would provide growth with protection – and lower taxes in retirement.

Premiums in: from age 42 thru 66 $60K yearly as annual payment

Initial death ben = $1.77 mil

Total in: $1.5 mil

IUL Performance Estimate = 7.5%

   (long tern historic average)

Distributions age 67 to 92 = $351K (tax free)

Cash value at end age 66 = $3.4 mil (tax free)	At 92 = 1.4 mil (tax free)
Death ben at end age 66 = $5.2 mil (tax free)	At 92 = $2.25 mil (tax free)

Comparison to a 401(k):

- assumed tax rate at retirement = 28%
- Performance in 401(k): assume 8.5% until age 66, then 5.5% after
- Distribute from age 67: equivalent amount to match after tax amount from IUL

Money runs out at age 82, and no death benefit.

Chapter 5

The "Secret Sauce" that Powers Superior Benefits

Hmmm...a NASCAR winner and the IUL? Both have been re-engineered and customized from humble beginnings to become superstars. A Toyota Camry, born a family type, became the recent Daytona 500 champ...

...while the IUL is also redesigned and modified from other, "stodgy" permanent policies to focus on cash accumulation and lengthy tax free distributions. How does it do that? It comes down to three critical "TLC" factors for: taxes, loans, and crediting strategies

1. **The "T" - tax breaks in the IRS codes regarding life insurance**

Often downplayed – even by financial professionals, is the fact that policyholders realize key tax advantages.

Specific tax advantages include:

- Tax deferral of gains as account grows
- Distributions– as loans are tax free – even above "cost basis" - if the IUL is designed in accordance with IRS codes 7702 and 72e
- Income Tax Free death benefit to heirs

"I can tell you that the single biggest benefit in the federal tax code is the income tax exemption for life insurance."

Ed Slott, tax advisor, was named "The Best Source for IRA Advice" by The Wall Street Journal and called "America's IRA Expert" by Mutual Funds Magazine. He is a nationally recognized IRA-distribution expert, professional speaker, and the creator of several public television specials.

2. The "L" – for loan provisions- are crucial and they enhance cash accumulation and duration of retirement income

   - The policy must be properly designed - including how and when premiums are paid so it is not considered a "Modified Endowment Contract" or MEC
   - Loans do not have to be repaid; will impact death benefit and cash values. Loans permit tax free distributions.
   - Most policies allow a "net zero" cost fixed rate loan
   - **Variable loan features - that vary by carrier - may allow you to earn money on amounts actually loaned out.** (Some carriers permit loans that do not come from your own account, but from the general account of the insurance carrier). This variable loan feature can add significantly to future income because it is possible to earn credits exceeding the loan rate.

   NOTE: Loans are not considered to be "income" so they are not "counted" in many important ways: as income in computing federal income taxes, AMT (the Alternate Minimum Tax), what's taxed on Social Security benefits, and college financial aid formulas

3. **The "C" – crediting strategies to build wealth – and provide protection.**

- Crediting strategies refer to what market indexes are used as basis for accumulating account values above policy premiums paid in and costs taken out. None of these involve a direct investment in an equity or index.

- The most common index is the S&P 500, a large company, diversified stock market benchmark, with an annual "point to point" method (from one point in time to another one year later). Dividends are excluded. Other strategies, from more conservative to more aggressive may be used.

- Annual gains, up to a cap, are locked in; gains are protected and cannot be lost due to market declines

4. **There's another "C" that's important– the IUL carrier**

The choice of carrier is a big deal!. Every carrier's IUL products entail differences regarding: crediting indexes and strategies, how and when monies are credited, policy fees and costs, type of loans and loan rate maximums, bonus credits, caps and floors, accelerated benefit provisions, a carrier's financial strength and more.

We *utilize third party, unbiased consumer-oriented data* to identify the "best" carriers in terms of how they fare on over twenty "deal-breaker and "deal-maker" factors and future cash values and income achievable.

Chapter 6

Who is Suitable for the IUL?

Is it any wonder that a tax free retirement savings solution is going to appeal predominantly to the affluent, right?

The answer is "not quite' because the IUL offers a package of benefits far beyond tax free income. Who the IUL should appeal to – and why – is described below:

A. the 'High end' of the Middle Class:

- Supplemental tax free income in retirement for this group (very dependent on Social Security) is quite important. Taking income – via loans – from one's IUL may prevent folks from going into a higher tax bracket.

- Market like returns and no market risk as well. Expected to provide more years of after tax spendable income than from an IRA or 401(k).

- May be able to save thousands on Social Security benefits. These benefits are taxable, but IUL loans do not count in formula for determining taxation. For high earners, saving on SS taxes is unlikely or small.

  Click http://tinyurl.com/SScalculate to see how you may save on taxes on your SS benefits. Note: income from loans on your IULs do not count in the formulas – but not the case when income comes from your 401(k) or IRA

- In pre-retirement years, there's very favorable access to your cash values using no or low cost loans that do not have to be repaid, Can be a superior method of taking common "consumer type loans" or for emergency needs vs credit cards or even bank loans. Some kinds of loans (variable) even permit earning excess monies on loaned out amounts.

- Accumulated funds do not count in college aid formulas – potentially allowing greater aid.

- The death benefit can be "accelerated" or advanced towards long term care expenses; long term care insurance often considered too expensive for middle income folks.

- The death benefit feature may be more important to this group in event of an early death.

B. **the "near affluent", affluent, or wealthy**

- A "no brainer": IULs offer tax free income for those who **can save the most - in an absolute sense - on taxes due to high marginal tax brackets.**

- Expected to provide more years of after tax income than from an IRA or 401(k) with comparable returns. May help one to be in lower tax bracket in retirement since IUL loans do not count as taxable income.

- Easy access (no penalties. taxes) to monies via no/ low interest loans; may utilize "positive arbitrage" to earn money on loaned out amounts (with some carriers). Able to take advantage of investment opportunities.

- No impact on AMT

- No income restrictions or contribution limits

- Accelerated benefits for long term care, terminal illness

- Includes a major life insurance benefit.

- NO Required Minimum Distributions (RMDs). Often, these are despised by those with assets in qualified plans where these monies are not needed and can add to one's legacy.

C. **for Small Business owners:**

- ALL factors as shown above for affluent. Plus:

- *The IUL is a private plan* – so there is no need for added expenses - such as contributions for employees or plan administration costs as with common business retirement plans

- NO government forms to complete (or associated costs)

- Privacy of transactions with respect to the IRS (as long as rules are followed in plan design)

- Creditor protection in some states

D. *Anyone with a Roth IRA – or who wanted one (but lost out because of income restrictions.*

Chapter 7

Why Consumers Don't Have a Clue (but totally should) About America's Best <u>Retirement Savings Solution</u>

Sadly, there remains **'Dirty Little Secrets' in how financial products are marketed** to consumers – and they are hardly aware of them. There's a long list of "culprits" including:

1. **Insurance companies**: You might expect that any company with a superior product would proclaim its benefits loud and clear. Perhaps surprisingly. IUL carriers do not do this. Why not?

   - the life carriers get some highly favorable tax breaks in the IRS codes including: tax deferred growth in account values, an income tax free death benefit, and the ability of policyholders to take out monies using tax free loans, above the cost basis (providing certain IRS rules are followed).

   - *While an opinion*, we believe that insurance companies are "concerned" that *marketing IULs as a viable investment strategy, with such tax favorable treatment might backfire and result in new, less favorable regulations.*

   - Something similar happened back in the 1980's; and three separate tax revenue related laws were passed which limited policy funding abuses (and reduced the use of life insurance as a tax shelter). <u>However, very favorable tax treatment still remains</u>.

2. **Insurance agents**: if employed by/contracted with certain major insurance carriers, they are *considered "captive" agents* and are expected to sell primarily their company's products – and are rewarded for doing so. "Rewards" range from continued employment, higher commissions, pension benefits, free vacations as incentives. *Consumers are probably not aware of this.*

   - **Many major carriers *do not even offer IULs*** (New York Life, Met, Northwestern, MassMutual, Guardian and others). These carriers typically offer whole life insurance product may not compare well with IULs in terms of potential future income Some of these *firms outright prohibit their agents from selling IULs.*

   - agents who work with firms where life insurance is not their primary business, such as Allstate, State Farm, Farmers – may have a very limited array of other carriers, who offer IULs, that they can sell from.

   - policy commissions vary from carrier to carrier – and agents may fare better advocating whole life or inferior IUL products and/or policy designs with carriers known to compensate better. Sometimes by a lot.

   - independent advisors most likely can provide clients with the widest array of options.

3. **Financial advisers** with investment management (brokerage) firms: typically, their advisors are less than expert about permanent life insurance. They get a very brief course (a few days) on life insurance early in their careers. Little follow up education; people sell what they know. They also have an equities "mindset" – and typically focus on fee based accounts (that in the long run, can be quite expensive).

   Most advisers do little sales of life insurance over their careers. Advisors will sometimes partner with experienced life agents from insurance carriers. *Further, their firms (broker-dealers) may have selling agreements with only a limited array of life carriers – and possibly not with carriers who offer IULs or the best rated ones.*

4. **CPAs** – these folks are tax experts - NOT insurance or investment professionals! *They may think they have this expertise; some may even be licensed. But,* this hardly constitutes the expertise to design the "right" IUL. CPAs tend to be conservative – and do not want to jeopardize their customer relationship. They may be reluctant to advocate a product based on limited expertise or fear causing more harm than good.

The BOTTOM LINE you need to know

Be very careful about who you trust to be your "Tax Free Retirement (IUL) Specialist". Your current trusted advisor/ agent/CPA – may serve you well in many ways – but maybe "not so much" when it comes to optimizing your lifetime tax free income and legacy.

So, what's at stake? You may risk:

- *not learning of IULs in the first place*

- *Presented with a non-optimal IUL plan design, using an insurance carrier with key IUL policy drawbacks. This can cut your future income in half or more – given the same premiums paid in!*

- *The 'wrong' plan design can also contribute to severe tax consequences when money is taken out.*

Chapter 8

14 Design Tips to Optimize Future Income

While it remains a life insurance product with a death benefit, many folks will use their IUL policy for its *supplemental (tax free) retirement income potential.*

How a policy is designed - the insureds age and health, policy features, crediting strategies, carrier used, etc. - will have a "huge" impact on future income distributed as policy loans. By "huge impact", we suggest that an optimally designed policy with many of the qualities noted below, can potentially double future income!

These guidelines are meant to give you some insider' tips' and a "fighting chance" to ensure your advisor considers them in designing the policy that's right for you

1. This one is huge! Use increasing death benefit option 2 (or B). This option will increase future income potential vs using the level benefit option 1 (or A). There are pros and cons of each which you need to discuss with your adviser.

2. Use variable loans if available. Variable loans (sometimes called 'participating') may have a significant impact on future income. These loans may be used after a certain number of years. However, conservative investors may forego some future income for greater safety - with a fixed rate.

3. Select a carrier with a maximum variable loan rate. Very important –because future interest rates may be quite higher than they are in 2016. Only a few carriers offer this.

4. When distributions are made, use the option - take out future income "all as loan, not "withdraw to basis, then loan" or other option. Money withdrawn does not earn future market credits, while money distributed as "loans" does participate in market gains.

5. Consider reducing the death benefit (if your prime concern is future income) when policy allows (often after 12 years); check with advisor and carrier. This reduction will reduce the costs of insurance that are part of all polices.

6. Select carrier with *most consumer friendly internal features*. We utilize an excellent third party unbiased resource: Brett Anderson, author, speaker and advisor. He's written a wonderful book: "<u>Last Chance Retirement</u>" and publishes a data-laden newsletter (IULdigest.com). Note this excerpt from "Last Chance Retirement" by Brett Anderson:

"All IULs are NOT alike! They range – based on past performance and future real expectations – from Dismal to Great! Why the difference? Because they all do have different caps, participation rates, costs, bonus (if any) and guarantees on them, fixed rate requirements, loan rate options and caps, minimum guaranties, accelerated or "advanced" benefits (terminal, chronic illnesses), and more. (In general the well "known companies have poorer IUL s because they can).

It is very difficult for an agent – let alone a lay person – to analyze (or even know what to analyze) to compare IUL's and have a sense of how they can be expected to really perform...

... how well an IUL may perform is also determined by how it is designed. To put together a well-designed IUL with a top co. *you must work with a financial advisor who knows and understands how to do this and who they are, and how the features and benefits compare to (all) the other companies in the market. Not many do.* If they provided you with this report then they likely do..."

7. Pay premiums annually vs monthly. Helps money grow a bit quicker.

8. Consider a Survivorship policy whereby no death benefit payment is made until both spouses are deceased. This potentially increases cash accumulation value.

9. Consider policy where one can select an extended payment arrangement of the death benefit to heirs. Typically, some minimal amount, such as 50% of the death benefit is paid out right away - with the balance paid out over a ten or longer year period. Only a handful of carriers allow this.

10. Depending on how "aggressive" vs. "conservative" you are as an investor – or your future market outlook - some crediting strategies may be more suitable for you. You should inquire of your advisor about products that offer index strategies that are suitable for you.

11. Consider putting in larger sums in shorter number of years, for example, in as little as 5 to 7 years, if possible. This can help a lot – and consider it if the assets to put in are available

12. Provide for regularly increasing premiums given expected rising income to "futurize" the IUL and permit greater future death benefits, cash accumulation and income distributed.

13. If there is a substantial difference in age of the spouses, *you might make the policy's insured the younger one.* This would, generally allow greater cash accumulation due to lower insurance costs. Of course, a death benefit would only be paid upon the younger spouse's death.

14. If the insured experiences a *change for the better "health-wise"*, consider applying for an improved underwriting rating. For example, becoming a non-smoker, attaining a more normal weight or a marked improvement in some disorder or condition – any of these might positively impact your insurance costs and this future income potential.

Curious what a personalized IUL illustration of your future income might look like? Contact the author at: steve.retirelikearockstar@gmail.com

Chapter 9

Beyond the IUL's 'basic' indexing strategy: conservative to aggressive alternatives

For the analytic and investment savvy types, this section is for you!

Crediting strategies for most IUL policies typically involve what is called the "annual point to point S & P 500 index" – perhaps three quarters or more choose that one - and for good reason:

- It's easy to explain
- Easy to track, and
- Actually, it's a fairly 'high performing' index, relative to others – especially in recent years

However, consumers crave choices – and there are many with the IUL. They range from the conservative to the aggressive – but there is no one strategy that will be best for all market scenarios.

Generally, carriers allow policyholders to allocate percentages to several strategies if they wish – in addition to the fixed interest rate. How often crediting strategies may be changed is up to the carrier.

Here's a discussion of nine other crediting strategies that may be suitable for you. Each of these will *have their own caps and potentially other conditions*. Only certain carriers will utilize these. (We do not disclose names of specific products/carriers on our public website).

Also, note that new products, with innovative crediting strategies appear on the scene frequently.

Conservative options

1. *"140% participation"* – *here the carrier will multiply the S & P 500 point to point – up to a cap of near 7-8% by 140%. Probably best for those who "foresee" limited future returns.*

2. *Dow Jones Industrial Average (DJIA, less dividends), annual point to point. Probably a bit more conservative than the S&P 500 as the Dow contains only 30 super high capitalization companies*

3. *"Performance trigger"* – *this concept may go by different names. Here, any return of 0.0% or higher will earn one a fixed percent of somewhere in the 6 to 8% area. Another fairly conservative option!*

4. *A Blend of US stocks and bonds from a leading international investment company using their proprietary strategy. Performance numbers in past 20 years are "excellent"*

5. *An optimized blend of US, Europe, and Hong Kong (China). After a one year "lookback" the top performing of the S&P, Euro 50 and Hang Seng is assigned 50% of the gain, the next one gets 30% of the gain and the last one gets 20%*

Aggressive

6. More risk oriented US indices, including the US Midcap and Russell (small company)

7. Foreign indices including a large company Europe index, the Nikkei (Japan) and the Hang Seng (China).

8. The S &P 500 using the Monthly Average approach. Based on monthly returns, the caps on this one can potentially result in an exceptionally high return if the market goes up fairly consistently throughout the year, as it did in 2013

9. There are a few carriers that offer some uncapped variations on an S&P 500 index – which under the right market conditions can produce huge returns (i.e. above 20%).

Typically these products will include **a "spread" or a threshold percentage that must be cleared first** for any gains to occur. That spread might be 4 to 6% - although for one carrier we know of, you can keep the first 7% before their 5% spread begins.... Then after the spread is met, you get all the remainder. (Dividends always excluded). Note that since 1995, the S&P 500 has exceeded 20% annual returns eight times.

IMPORTANT NOTES

1. Any values paid out, for any policy, are based on the claims paying ability of the carrier. Policies are not

FDIC insured although carriers are regulated at the state level.

2. All policies involve expenses and fees which are subtracted from account values regardless of any index performance.

3. Carriers may offer bonus credits – over and above normal crediting of a strategy selected.

4. Generally, dividends paid on the indices are excluded from credits paid.

5. Carriers may vary the timing of crediting accounts with market linked credits

6. A particular strategy, however appealing, should be only one of many factors to consider in evaluating the suitability of a product/carrier for you.

7. Carriers have the right to modify caps and floors;/ may alter crediting strategies

8. Carries may increase their internal costs, which would impact future performance.

Chapter 10

Show Me the Money: IUL Funding Sources

Let's assume you are 'intrigued' by what the IUL can offer, but wonder: "where do I get the money to pay the premiums?" Here's some thoughts on where you might look.

Some 'obvious' sources

- Money being saved or kept liquid in low yielding bank accounts, including CDs, money market, or savings accounts
- Funds that might normally be earmarked for IRA or Roth accounts
- Contributions for a 401(k) in excess of what will be matched
- Funds in low returning fixed annuities

Less obvious sources

- Assets (some % of them) at risk in equity type accounts

- Cash values in permanent life policies – although great care must be established to make sure a "replacement" – into an IUL - is suitable and in your best interests. These policies may be whole life or 'regular' (non-indexed) universal life.

- Assets that may be in Section 529 College Savings plans. Depending on potential taxes, penalties

33

and ages of the children – making withdrawals to contribute to a IUL *might make sense.*

- Funds that might be freed up from a change in one's mortgage situation.

Chapter 11

Why Women (Should) Embrace This
New Retirement Plan Alternative

Special retirement challenges females face...

Sadly, while the prospect of living a financially secure retirement eludes many – it is a special challenge for women in particular. The good news: there's a retirement savings strategy that can be just the solution needed. What are those special challenges that women face?

Some recent survey results

The Transamerica Center for Retirement Studies®, using the Harris Poll group, conducted a 2015 national survey of thousands of male and female U.S. workers regarding their attitudes toward retirement. Some key findings:

1. Few Women Are Very Confident About Retirement
2. Most Women Plan to Retire After Age 65 or Not at All
3. Half of Women Plan to Continue Working in Retirement
4. Most Baby Boomer Women Don't Have a Backup Plan
5. Many Women Plan to Self-Fund Their Retirement
6. Most Have Concerns About the Future of Social Security
7. Time Off – and Costs - for Caregiving (Parents or Spouse) Will Impact Retirement

8. Many Women Work Part-Time (with lesser access to retirement plans)
9. Women's Participation Lags in 401(k) or Similar Plans
10. Most Women Are Saving Outside of Work
11. Women Estimate They Will Need $1 Million
12. Women Are Guessing Their Retirement Savings Needs

This adds up to concerns galore – but remember, we did say there was good news! We've previously touched upon the basics, and the many benefits of that fairly new, yet largely unknown kind of retirement savings solution (the IUL).

Here's the "special" benefits of IULs that women should love...

The issues/features that would seem to have a *special appeal to women* include:

1. **Longer lasting retirement assets** - given greater longevity, generally by several years. Women may have an even greater need for longer term retirement assets because they may incur expenses for the care of a spouse or partner. The death of a spouse will also reduce their Social Security income. Well-designed IULs from top carriers can be shown to produce more after tax, spendable income than from a comparable IRA or 401(k).

   Further, females engender lower mortality costs which all things being equal, will result in higher lifetime income possible than for males.

2. ***Maximized Social Security (SS) benefits*** – Income from IUL loans do not count in formulas for determining taxation of your SS benefits. Income from your IRAs and 401(k)'s do count.

   See how this can help you by clicking on this link: http://tinyurl.com/SScalculate Income from IUL's vs IRA's can amount to saving thousands annually. There's a case study example of this on our website (www.integrityincomesolutions.com)

3. ***Long term care (LTC)*** coverage – alluded to earlier, the need for such care becomes almost a certainty for a majority of those who make it to 80 and beyond. LTC insurance is expensive, is subject to rate increases - and is avoided by most. *The better IUL policies allow one to advance or "accelerate" t*he death benefit (usually about 20% or more of it annually) to pay for these costs... which can be enormous. If this area is of particular concern, it argues for both spouses to have an IUL policy.

4. ***Easy, penalty and tax free loans*** *i*f funds needed, anytime, for any reason. "Be your own bank!"

5. ***Risk tolerance*** – Women tend to be somewhat more risk averse than men. IULs, while they have costs, allow market linked gains, *but incur no risk (losses) due to market downturns.*

6. ***The death benefit*** (*hey, the IUL is a life insurance policy!*) can sure come in handy for providing for final expenses, debts and continuation of income in the event of an untimely death of a spouse or partner. A disability can also result in major hits to one's retirement funds.

While folks are primarily drawn to the IUL for the supplemental tax free income in retirement – the fact is that so many are under insured, particularly in years they are not employed and getting their company's group term insurance.

When you add it all up – for the right person – and women in particular - this strategy is tough to beat. Sadly, the surprising fact is that so few are aware of this. Why is this? We refer to this as "What consumers don't know about the dirty little secrets of marketing financial products" We've got a blog on that too.

Late breaking (June 2016) Just came across this article (excuse the long link!):

"Dire straits for women and retirement preparedness"

http://www.benefitspro.com/2016/06/22/dire-straits-for-women-and-retirement-preparedness?eNL=5 76b15bb140ba0bb1e5c33e5&utm_source=BPro_ RetirementAdvisorPro&utm_medium=EMC-Email_ editorial&utm_campaign=06232016

Chapter 12

IUL Costs: Is the 'Bad Press' justified?

In the market for a car? Checking out a Jetta or a Jaguar? How about a Kia or a Cadillac? Which of each pair is the least costly? That's easy. How about "Which one is *the better value*"?

"Costs are only important in the absence of value"

We don't know who said this... but you get the point.

It's fair to say that most "haters" of using cash value insurance *for any purpose* will point to high costs as a reason to avoid these. The same folks either

- *do not understand how the IULs work* (i.e. the means by which they produce incredible after tax income for lengthy periods of time – or

- they *market a competitor product such as "whole life" (WL) permanent insurance.* If that advisor works for an investment management (broker-dealer) firm, they often advocate managed, fee based equity accounts instead.

The "old guard" insurance carriers are in "attack mode"

You should know that many long established insurance carriers that market "whole life" (WL) policies do not offer the IUL – and they forbid their agents from selling it! Interestingly,

WL sales are stagnating while IUL sales are booming. The "debate" between IUL vs WL advocates will rage for a long time. However, it is beyond our scope here and now to say too much beyond the following:

- WL is *a guarantee focused, level premium product* and is more intended for someone who has low risk tolerance, wants guarantees and is willing to forego cash value and future income potential (given the same premiums put in) as possible with the IUL.

- WL costs may be substantially higher – and are very difficult to see spelled out clearly (which is done by IUL policies). Should you have one of these –or are now considering one we "challenge" you to ask your agent to tell you what all their costs are!

- *A "good" IUL policy may provide potentially twice the future income as a WL given the same premium.*

What are the IUL charges and fees?

There are typically four different charges deducted from the cash value of an Indexed UL policy. Two of those charges (a Premium Load Charge and a Monthly Charge per $1,000 of Death Benefit) are, essentially, sales charges – somewhat analogous to the transaction fees or management fees that one might pay to money managers, brokers, or investment advisors.

The Premium Load Charge (often between 5 and 7% of annual premium) is assessed each time a premium is paid. A Monthly Charge per $1,000 of Death Benefit is only assessed (usually) for the first 10 years after the policy is issued. The third charge is a generally nominal (perhaps $75 annually) Annual Expense charge. The fourth charge, the Monthly Cost of Insurance per $1,000 of Death Benefit, is the mortality charge associated with providing the policy's death benefit – and this is the only charge that is scheduled to increase each year.

Cost of insurance and age: what you really need to know

However, this last charge, for "Cost of Insurance" is often misunderstood – even by professionals. Insurance carriers do not base the COI on the amount of the death benefit per se – but instead on the "net amount at risk to the carrier" which can be defined as the death benefit minus the cash accumulation value in the account. Upon death, the beneficiary receives only the death benefit. Since IULs gain substantial cash value over time, while *the COI rate* (for someone of a given sex and age) will rise, *the actual amount of COI tends to level off.*

Lastly, some carriers help offset rising costs by offering added index credits, sometimes called "bonus credits", above and beyond the IULs index credits, to one's account value. This may be in the 0.75% to 1% area after the tenth year.

Cost vs benefit: this is easy with the IUL

While the IUL has significant early costs:

- They *go down substantially over time*, which is not true of equity based, mutual fund or wrap fee accounts (as balances rise). Mutual fund charges and the totality of possible 401(k) expenses are far larger than most expect – and these 'high' charges last a lifetime. Again, insurance expenses and charges decline markedly after the tenth year.

-   The IUL's long term after tax spendable income advantage vs what's available from other retirement accounts (IRAs, 401k) is considerable and provable too.

-   Additional, less obvious valuable benefits can be substantial, such as for reduced or eliminated taxes for *Social Security benefits* and the *ability to earn monies on loaned out amounts.*

-   There is some value to having life insurance coverage per se; this is not free. And, the paid out death benefit - unlike a 401(k) or IRA balance – is income tax free.

-   Difficult to value IUL "intangibles" such as the "sleep well at night' factor one gets with the "no risk" nature of a "zero floor" can be a real blessing! There is never a loss due to a falling market. So, this safety net can keep one "in the market" in your IUL. Whereas someone near or in retirement in an equity based account may feel the need to re-allocate significant percentages to low yielding money market or fixed investments.

Chapter 13

Full Disclosure: Drawbacks and Disclaimers

All financial products or strategies have downsides; are not right for all persons at all times.

We believe it's only fair to disclose the negatives of any financial solution. Some downsides will be a deal-breaker; others one can "live with" given the totality of benefits. Let's take a look:

1. **No tax deductions of premiums.** For some, this alone might be a deal-breaker. However, the numerous long term advantages – and tax free income in retirement – help mitigate this issue. Answer this:

   "If you were a farmer, would you rather pay taxes on the seed or the harvest?"

2. **There is life insurance underwriting.**

   This will require a review of your medical history – and other variables deemed relevant to mortality.

   - The underwriting review results *in a health "rating"* – which can vary from "super good health" or "preferred" to poor ratings to "uninsurable". The rating has a major impact on your costs of insurance and thus how your IUL will perform.

- *With good health*, the good news is that this rating gets locked in forever – despite future health changes.

- For those *with poorer ratings*, costs will be higher. However, consider 2 options: A) you may apply for a better rating in subsequent years if there is improvement in an important health factor. B) utilize a IUL policy with a spouse or partner, as the insured one, who is in better health or significantly younger. The policy owner CONTROLS payments and how income is taken out.

3. **Costs and fees**. This is often the "big knock" on cash value policies.

No doubt, IUL policies are "front loaded" - costs are high during the first ten years. That percent (of premiums put in) may be in the 20 to 25% area.

However, IUL costs decline dramatically afterwards – The duration of these lower IUL fees can well last 30 to 40 years depending on life expectancy.

Some IUL policies employ a HIGH EARLY CASH VALUE feature which eliminates premium expenses and surrender charges - something of interest in business insurance (bonus compensation) scenarios

Looking at costs for other retirement approaches, note that equity/mutual fund/managed account fees rise as time goes by and assets accumulate. The true costs of mutual funds are quite a bit higher than one sees in the "expense ratio". And, admin fees and other costs of your 401(k) act to decrease your assets over time as well.

Bottom line: over the long term, IUL costs are substantially lower than alternatives.

4. **Long term focus crucial**. Taking on an IUL policy is a long term strategy best requiring 12 to 15 or more years. If you do not have this sort of time frame, an IUL is not suitable for you.

5. **The S&P 500 index used does not include dividends**. Dividends would add perhaps 1.5% to the index return. Of course, the IUL has a 'zero floor" to help mitigate that. And, some carriers offer bonus index credits at some time after the policy has been in force.

6. **Index caps can change**. True, but the history – over the past 15 years - has been one of fairly stable index caps in the 12 to 15% area. Since the "cap" is partly related to interest rates – and near record lows in the early 2016, there is a good chance that caps will remain near where they are now - or even rise.

7. **Surrender charges**. Should one give up, "cash out" or "surrender" the policy, generally in the first 10 to 15 years, there is a steep penalty charge (gets lower as you approach the end of the surrender period).

8. The **IUL "Guarantee" columns** on a carrier's illustration shows a major reduction of values over time and the policy ending.

   The problem with this is: all the assumptions are so unlikely, including: charging the maximum possible on costs (typically, costs have gone down as mortality has improved etc.), and the market never going up!

Such a scenario would wreak havoc on any equity based account as well – where losses would count and be devastating.

Anyone who requires "guarantees" might prefer a whole life policy or other, fixed investments

9. The IUL is "too complicated"

Yes, it is complicated with lots of moving parts! So are many high tech devices, sports cars etc. "Complicated" doesn't mean "bad".

The website, our resources – including the opportunity to communicate with us – are intended to "un-complicate" this.

Chapter 14

In Closing: The Retirement Challenges

For most Americans, their biggest fears are things like snakes, heights, speaking in public (yes, this is a big one).

However, for those facing retirement, that #1 fear is "outliving your money". Each of the factors discussed below relates to those fears. And, perhaps not surprisingly - when you have all the facts – a retirement solution using the IUL addresses ALL of them better than any traditional retirement plan.

1. **Longevity.** This is both the good news and bad news! Today, the fastest growing segments of the population are those in the 80's, 90's and beyond! Living a good life for so many years in retirement can be a major financial challenge.

   The IUL 'answer:' – policy provisions, no risk crediting strategies and loan features make IULs provide more years of income given com parable market conditions

2. **Taxes.** Think your taxes are headed lower when you retire? Most Americans think, if anything, rates are headed up. Our huge debt makes it likely future tax rates will rise.. Believe it or not – tax rates have occasionally exceeded 90%!

   The IUL 'answer' – you pay no income taxes on distributions. And, for many, you'll pay less taxes on your Social Security benefits which alone can be in the thousands of dollars yearly.

3. **Inflation**. Fairly low in recent years… but many have also lived through rates several times higher. Even a "low" rate of 3% will double costs in 24 years.

   The IUL 'answer' – market like crediting strategies, over time tend to outperform inflation rates.

4. **Market volatility**. Markets go up and then sometimes down, down, and down. If at the "wrong time" – such as near or in retirement, market losses can be devastating. So, to "stay the course" and keep invested in equities – as advisors/brokers tell you to do, can prove difficult to maintain. Yet, re-allocating to very conservative, safe investments can wreak havoc to returns.

   The IUL 'answer' – beyond "sleeping well at night", IUL account values cannot decline due to market declines. There are some carriers where the floor is 1 or 2%. Further, with zero market risk, one can maintain the indirect market participation which can result in greater long term returns than from fixed rate options or fixed income investments in your qualified plan (i.e. IRA)

5. **Health issues**. The cost of care can be enormous and devastate one's assets. However, many shy away from costly long term care insurance which can prove very helpful.

The IUL 'answer' – being able to 'advance' the death benefit towards long term care expenses (or critical care expenses) can make a big difference in a family's financial picture – especially in the absence of having LT care insurance, which few have.

There is ONE retirement solution that helps deal with all the above… and it's the IUL.

Chapter 15

Next steps

a. *How to Choose Your IUL Advisor*

To design an optimal IUL, you need someone with a combination of expertise, independence and integrity. Any element missing here can result in a plan design not maximized for your future income and legacy... sometimes by a lot.

Many of your current advisors may serve you well on a number of fronts .... But if they do not possess the above 3 qualities, if they are not a *specialist* in this, what you're offered will fall short of what's possible.

b. "You don't buy this on Amazon".

Hey, Amazon IS great...but the IUL is simply not something you buy this way. Human, expert "intervention" is needed and critical

c. "Who you gonna' call?" (little joke; not Ghostbusters!)

OK, we hope it's us.

The author's contact information:

Email: steve.retirelikearockstar@gmail.com

Phone no. Toll free 844.766.8297.

Web site (under construction; should be open by Mar 15, 2025):
www.retireandlivelikearockstar.com

ps. You may contact the author for:

- a free, no obligations 20 minute "discovery" call or screen share
- a no obligations "estimate" of what an IUL plan can look like (called an "illustration") for you including anticipated lifetime tax free income starting at retirement

About the Author

The author, Steve Dravin has a Masters Degree in Organizational Psychology from the University of Illinois and has had careers in Human Resources Training and Development as well as in Financial Services focusing on equity products and insurance. He has worked for several major brokerage houses and insurance firms since 1992.

I have come to know a broad array of investment products – and realize some of the challenges inherent in doing right by clients – when your livelihood is at stake.

The author's basic philosophy is that selling should be more about educating clients about what is right for them and what they are comfortable with. Then, let them choose. Yet, many of his peers succumb to the pressure of sales – and frankly, do not do right by many.

The purpose of writing "Retire Like a Rock Star" was to inform folks about a relatively unknown, yet very worthwhile kind of "retirement plan" – because most would not have even heard of it for a surprising series of reasons. Those reasons are detailed in one of the chapters. But, real quick - many advisors are simply not allowed to sell it! Many financial firms do not even offer it. And conflicts over how advisors earn their income make the IUL a product that will often not be offered – even when it accomplishes so many things.

We hope you will be open to learning about something that can truly change your life! Hopefully, while this book will not make you an IUL expert, it will give you enough "ammunition" to make sure your advisor (perhaps yours truly) makes the effort to get you the best plan possible.

Printed in the United States
by Baker & Taylor Publisher Services